Ketogenic Diet:

How to Achieve Rapid and Permanent Weight Loss, Increase Mental Clarity and Lessen Side Effects, Plus 38 Recipes

By Kate Dawson

© Copyright 2016 - All rights reserved.

In no way is it legal to reproduce, duplicate, or transmit any part of this document in either electronic means or in printed format. Recording of this publication is strictly prohibited and any storage of this document is not allowed unless with written permission from the publisher. All rights reserved.

The information provided herein is stated to be truthful and consistent, in that any liability, in terms of inattention or otherwise, by any usage or abuse of any policies, processes, or directions contained within is the solitary and utter responsibility of the recipient reader. Under no circumstances will any legal responsibility or blame be held against the publisher for any reparation, damages, or monetary loss due to the information herein, either directly or indirectly.
Respective authors own all copyrights not held by the publisher.

Legal Notice:

This book is copyright protected. This is only for personal use. You cannot amend, distribute, sell, use, quote or paraphrase any part or the content within this book without the consent of the author or copyright owner. Legal action will be pursued if this is breached.

Disclaimer Notice:

Please note the information contained within this document is for educational and entertainment purposes only. Every attempt has been made to provide accurate, up to date and reliable complete information. No warranties of any kind are expressed or implied. Readers acknowledge that the author is not engaging in the rendering of legal, financial, medical or professional advice.

By reading this document, the reader agrees that under no circumstances are we responsible for any losses, direct or indirect, which are incurred as a result of the use of information contained within this document, including, but not limited to; errors, omissions, or inaccuracies.

Table of Contents

Introduction 1

Chapter 1: An Outline of the Ketogenic Diet 2

Chapter 2: What to Avoid on The Diet 6

Chapter 3: Important Factors and Side Effects of the Diet 10

Chapter 4: The Must Have Grocery List 15

Chapter 5: Yummy Breakfast Recipes 25

Chapter 6: Awesome Salads 37

Chapter 7: Beautiful Main Meals 48

Chapter 8: Tempting Snacks & Desserts 62

Conclusion 75

Introduction

The Ketogenic Diet, or as everyone is calling it the Keto Diet has made some headway recently. How does it work? This is a question you may be thinking, and it's true that not all diets are the same. Do you reduce precious calories and do more exercise? In most cases, yes, but this one puts that theory on its head. I can tell you freely that exercise should still be a part of this diet just like any other, but the way it works is way different to most of the other diets you may have read about. Without delving into too much detail right now, it is basically a very low carbohydrate diet with those amounts being replaced with fat! Oh yes, you heard me correctly - and I will explain this in further detail later on. Although with most diets, there are a few downsides and side effects that I must tell you about too, but for now I will just let you know. This diet doesn't just help you lose weight, it does even more in many cases. I have seen lots of health benefits that come by following the Keto Diet, and some studies are being conducted by some of the major medical institutions and natural therapists right around the world.

Chapter 1: An Outline of the Ketogenic Diet

As I mentioned previously, the Keto diet consists of a very low carbohydrate intake which is replaced by fat. So, contrary to what you would expect to happen by increasing your fat content, by decreasing your carb intake at the same time forces your body into a metabolic state that is known as ketosis. In this state, your body has lower amounts of glucose to convert to energy, so it turns to fat that is stored in the body. The body reacts and this is where it becomes highly efficient at converting that fat into energy. The ketones produced have special properties; they are a direct replacement for glucose which gives energy to the brain, a place where fatty acids cannot be used.

It has been proven, that people following this diet have had reduced blood sugar and insulin levels and I forgot to mention to you, that all of this and what follows takes place without you feeling hungry (like you would on just a calorie reduced diet). At present, I have researched there to be 4 types of Ketogenic Diets, but the two most widely studied are the *Standard Ketogenic Diet (SKD)* and the *High Protein Ketogenic Diet*, the final 2 are a lot more involved - and are normally followed by body builders and athletes. So from here on, I will just be focusing clearly upon the *Standard Ketogenic Diet*.

Well, let's talk about diabetes, because we know this is a change in metabolism. Additionally, your body's insulin production state is not up to par here. The presence of type 2 diabetes is directly linked to excessive body fat, and it is here the Ketogenic diet can help you lose those extra pounds and lower the risks, occurring fundamentally from type 2.

There are various studies showing the benefits of the Keto diet for people who have diabetes, without overwhelming you with too many details, there are reports of people who have been able to reduce or stop their medication all together. Even more promising is that other tests report some people on the Keto diet were able to lose nearly double the amount of weight. That is compared to people on a regular higher carb diet.

The thing I find remarkable is you do not have to count calories like most other diets, this gives you the opportunity to eat more and become more satisfied between meals. This in turn helps remove that temptation just to have a nibble of something. I was astonished when I found out the Keto diet is not a new thing, it was actually designed 90 years ago, and was originally designed to help relieve epilepsy. After a few years, its popularity waned as new epilepsy drugs were coming onto the market.

It started to become popular again around 1994, when a young man named Charlie Abraham made a complete recovery from severe seizures that he was suffering on a daily basis. It was at this point his family started, *"The Charlie Foundation."* They tried the Keto Diet, after they had tried all anti-seizure products, to no avail. Charlie was only a child when he started following this diet, and remained on it for 5 years until his seizures stopped. Up until this day, *The Charlie Foundation* is a global leader in the promotion of Ketogenic therapies.

Now to a bit more of the nitty gritty you need to know, because there are a few things you should and need to know before starting on the Keto Diet. Should you seek medical supervision? Yes, you should. All foods should be carefully weighed and prepared and all of the prepared meals should be eaten for the full effect to happen.

There are two forms of the classic diet, with the only minor difference being the amount of fat compared to that of non-fat, which would be proteins and carbohydrates. There is the 3:1 ratio and the 4:1 ratio diet.

It has been widely acknowledged that children who have seizures can benefit most, all the way from infancy up until their teenage years; most believe the reasoning for this is that children are more reliant on adults to provide for them at this stage in their lives. Over the past few years, there have been more creative recipes that appeal to children, and test results in every decade since the 1920's show: that the number of cases in children that have seizures has reduced dramatically, some being as much as 50% - 75%.

I can see you are wondering what about dining out, well this can be a lot easier than you may think, most restaurants offer meals consisting of meat or fish dishes. So, if there is anything in your meal that consists of high carbohydrates - just replace this with more vegetables.

If you are dining at lunch time, another option you have can be a simple omelette or bacon and eggs. Choose a bun-less burger and just swap the fries for vegetables, or have the burger with bacon and eggs and extra cheese. Desserts can consist of a simple, mixed cheese board or berries (strawberries etc.) served with double cream.

I have spoken to a lot of people who think that when a body is in a state of "ketosis" this is dangerous, and it does sound that way but let me reassure you, all this means is your body is starting to burn the fat deposits that are to be converted to energy. In this state, the ketones generated are molecules that are being produced during the body's burning of its fat deposits.

When you reduce and eat fewer carbohydrates, your body will naturally turn to fat deposits for energy, with some of the ketones getting used for energy and others going to improving your heart and kidney functioning, as they prefer ketones rather than glucose to operate. For many normal people, the average time for their body to reach a state of ketosis is about 4 – 6 weeks.

We all know most diets involve a change in your lifestyle and as with will all diets: there are downsides and things to avoid, things we should do, and things we shouldn't do. Hopefully, if we work together we can make this change easier to come to terms with, especially in the first few weeks when you start your path to becoming a slimmer, healthier and a more energized you. Not just for now, but for many years to come.

Chapter 2: What to Avoid on The Diet

At all costs, you should not just adopt the Keto Diet if you have any medical problems or are a serious athlete whose daily intake would be very different to regular person's, due to the extra fitness regime and calorie intake required to promote muscle. Another group of people who should seek medical supervision are ones who are prone to kidney stones and gout. Always seek medical advice if you are unsure, because your health is vitally important, always.

As mentioned previously, there are things that you must avoid while undertaking the Keto diet, so here I will try and explain in simple terms what foods and drinks you should try to avoid. And not just when your body is in a state of ketosis, but while you are adjusting to getting your body into this state, including what can bring your body out of the ketosis state without you being aware. It is better to follow these guides now, rather than realize all of your hard work is not giving you the complete health benefits you deserve.

Although protein is not to be avoided whilst on the Keto diet, it has to be eaten in moderation, as a high intake can raise your insulin levels and at the same time lower your ketone levels. Therefore, an approximate amount of protein on a daily basis should be about 35% maximum (of your total calorie intake for that day).

As previously mentioned, the Keto diet is a low carb high fat diet, but not all fats are suitable as they have many different effects on the body, and the body's metabolism. A lot of studies conducted have come to the consensus to avoid where possible any oils that are high in polyunsaturated (omega 6) fats. The most common of these are: corn, soy, cottonseed, and safflower amongst others. Additionally, a common source for these types of oils are salad dressings and more commonly mayonnaise.

Unlike the oils mentioned, the following items which are to be avoided are more common and easier to identify. After reading, you will probably realize these are some of the downsides to the Keto diet, if not the major downsides. Some of these are the items that are most accessible for our modern feeding habits, and also the things that we enjoy most.

Believe it or not *"Sugar-Free Diet Foods"* need to be avoided, as these are normally very highly processed and they often possess high levels of sugar alcohols. Actually, these in some cases can affect ketone levels quite dramatically, in some people.

Low fat or diet products, as with the *Sugar-Free Diet Foods*, are normally highly processed - and high in carbohydrates. Examples can consist of diet soda, chewing gum and mints. If they do not contain a high level of carbs, there is a good chance they will contain some levels of gluten.

Alcohol (which is basically made from grains), can have a high carb content, so this can place the body out of line with the wanted ketosis state. Condiments, ketchups and sauces; these normally contain high levels of unhealthy fats and high levels of sugar and other additives. This is because the majority of them are highly processed. Root vegetables are one of the most common types of foods which we consume in our normal diets, and unfortunately, they contain some of the highest amounts of carbs, as well. A few of the most common are: potatoes, carrots, sweet potatoes and parsnips. Avoidance of these, therefore, is necessary.

Grains and starches are also to be avoided on the Keto diet, and most meals throughout the day can consist of these in one form or another. From breakfast, lunch, dinner and supper. The main items that you should avoid are wheat based cereals, rice, and pastas. If you are unsure where these items are used, the following items will probably make you sigh! I will highlight what to look out for: breads, pizza, cookies and crackers.

Sugary foods and drinks, (I can imagine you are thinking this is getting worse!) There is nothing left to eat or drink, but I will get to that later; for now, I need to tell you the hard facts. Sodas, fruit Juices, ice cream, cake, and candy should all be avoided.

Some fruits are to be avoided. Dried Fruits (raisins, dates etc.), tropical fruits like pineapple, mango, bananas and others. Some others are high in carbs too, like tangerines and grapes. Berries like strawberries can be eaten. You can search foods with low carbs or no carbs online.

Beans and legumes are other staple items in our diet, but chickpeas, lentils, kidney beans and peas are also on the hit list of those that should be avoided.

Fresh milk should be avoided or taken in moderation. Although milk is good for us, we are told it contains calcium for strong bones. This is true but as it is normally pasteurized - all the good bacteria have been eliminated and it is actually quite hard for your body to digest, in most cases. Secondly, something you may not realize is, it actually contains a high amount of carbohydrates. So, if you are drinking tea or coffee, it is advisable to use a small amount of cream as a replacement.

Even though they are used to replace sugar, artificial sweeteners should be avoided as they can induce cravings and there are no health benefits due to them being fully processed. Factory farmed meats and fish can contain high amounts of Omega 6 fatty acids, and factory farmed fish may contain Polychlorinated Biphenyls or PCBs for short - which are manmade and hazardous to health. This is because they are transferred up the food chain and can even be passed on to breastfeeding babies, which are at risk from these.

Although not directly linked to affecting the Keto diet, there are some things that should be avoided just for health reasons. Soy products which are not fermented, carrageenan which can be found in almonds and coconut milk products. It is used as a thickener/ stabilizer and in MSG, which is included in processed foods as a flavor enhancer.

Chapter 3: Important Factors and Side Effects of the Diet

There are a few side effects and factors that I need to make you aware of, these can differ if the Keto diet is for children or for adults. Most of these are quite manageable if you come to understand what makes them happen. You can minimize them so you are not inclined to quit before you start to reap the benefits of the diet, too.

It only takes a few weeks for your body to enter a ketosis state; from this point forward most side effects will start to subside, as your body has adapted to burning fat for energy rather than glucose. For your benefit, I have compiled a list of the most common side effects and what you can do to cope with them. Please always, always seek medical advice before you start. Be health minded for safety, and long term longevity.

Low Blood Sugar (Hypoglycemia)

As your body is normally used to a higher carb diet, it creates insulin to counteract the amount of sugar that gets created from all the carbohydrate intake. Once your carb quantity drops on the Keto diet, it is possible you can experience some low blood sugar episodes, and if not experienced before can seem quite scary. An effective way to maintain this is to buy some glucose tablets - and when you feel this happening, just take one or two tablets and this should subside. Seek medical or pharmacy advice here if you need to.

Headaches

As with any major change in diet, headaches can manifest for no apparent reason, it is possible you may become light headed, and also start to have flu-like symptoms which will occur over a few days. These headaches normally happen because of a mineral imbalance due to a diet change. One way to resolve this quickly is to add one-quarter of a teaspoon of salt into a glass of water and drink. Then you should sit down as this can take around twenty minutes before its effects take place. At the start of your diet, you should increase both your salt and water intake for the first few days, to combat this effectively.

Fatigue and Dizziness

As mentioned above, as your body starts to lose its stored water content, you have to make sure this is replaced, as a result, there are many minerals that will be lost as a you go along. With a low level of these minerals, it can cause you to feel tired, dizzy and lightheaded and also make it possible to get unwanted muscle cramps - and a possibility of itchy skin. To help combat these effects, an increased amount of green leafy vegetables is recommended, it is also possible to use multivitamin tablets that provide the recommended daily allowance for the minerals that you require. Stay clear of the vegetables that are high in carbs, discussed earlier, though.

Constipation

This is one of those that no one wants to talk about, although it is one of the most common side effects. This comes about by dehydration, loss of salt, a magnesium deficiency or too much dairy/nut products. If things do not change with the vitamin tablets (to improve your magnesium intake), you may have to reduce your dairy product intake even more, at this point.

Diarrhea

The complete opposite of constipation - and this one is something that most people do not like to mention. Although as we all know, it can be quite drastic when it happens, but these symptoms normally only last for a few days, thankfully. Once you have increased your fat content, your body should adjust and these symptoms should subside. Always be mindful of drinking lots of water to replace the lost fluid, at this time.

Interrupted Sleep Patterns

I have heard people mention they have problems sleeping when they are on the Keto diet - and if this happens it can be a sign you have low insulin levels. A solution to this is to have a small snack which contains an equal amount of protein and carbohydrate, just before you go to bed. This should help balance your insulin level for the night. Just for the short term.

Heart Palpitations

This is one of those things that can happen to some people, and not happen to others, like when drinking a strong cup of coffee. Although while on the Keto diet it could be a sign of a person that normally has low blood pressure. Always seek medical advice if you are not sure.

Sugar Cravings

This is the one we all love to hate, it shows us our weak spot and is one of the most difficult side effects to resist. But I beg you to just give it time - and these will subside in anything from a few days up to a period of around 21 days. A few ways to combat this, is by doing some light exercise, or finding something that will totally occupy your mind. Sugar cravings normally only last for an hour; this will have subsided by the time you have completed your task. It is also possible to have a snack consisting of a few ounces of protein, either in the form of a small salad or a small, quick to prepare smoothie.

These are some of the most common occurrences of side effects which most people have reported, through studies that have been conducted. Additionally, there are also reports of people having the following side effects:

Hair loss – this is not directly linked to the Keto diet, but just to a complete change in diet.

Low Thyroid T3 Hormone levels – this happens in most reduced calorie diets; it is an effect of the body's reduced calorie intake.

If the Keto diet is followed for a long duration, there are a few different side effects that may arise and may affect children much more than adults. It should NEVER be used on children.

Kidney Stones – these can affect children more commonly than adults; it is estimated there is a 5% possibility a child could have kidney stones after following the diet.

Stunted Growth – this can be a problem for children as there is a reduced amount of growth factor 1 hormone. Along with stunted growth, there is a risk of bone fractures due to the reduced amounts of growth factor 1 hormone.

Again, NEVER place a child on a ketogenic diet, because the consequences are very drastic and harmful. Children are still growing, so give them all the fruits, vegetables, carbs and proteins, in a balanced diet. Limit their processed sugar found in candy, sodas and sweets.

Chapter 4: The Must Have Grocery List

As with most diets, it is necessary to change your shopping habits and also change the ingredients in your kitchen, the Keto diet is no exception. The list below is not complete as that would probably fill more than the whole of this book. The aim of this is just to give a good understanding and a starting point of what is available and what you should be avoiding. The best advice is to eat a variety of fresh meat, wild caught seafood, plenty of fresh vegetables and natural fats which have not been processed. If used in moderation, some canned goods can be used, as long as they are not processed meals.

Pantry Items

Beef Jerky

Pork Rinds

Sugar-free salad dressings

Hot sauces

Canned tomatoes (be sure to check the carbohydrate content)

Canned sauces (make sure there is no thickeners or added sugar)

Canned fish

Chicken or vegetable stock

Apple cider and wine vinegar

Nut butter (make sure they are unsweetened and natural)

Low carbohydrate vegetables: green beans, sauerkraut, and okra (with no added sugar)

Lemon or lime juice (contains 1 gram of carbohydrate per tablespoon)

Horseradish

Salsas (check contents to find one that is suitable)

Pickles (which are sugar-free)

Natural mustard (sweetened mustards not to be used)

Capers

Cooking and Baking Ingredients

Nut flour

Flour substitutes

Cooking oil (coconut oil and peanut oil are suitable)

Unsweetened extracts (almond, vanilla and lemon etc.)

Whey protein powder (chocolate, plain, and vanilla flavors)

Unsweetened cocoa powder

Herbs & Spices

You should experiment with herbs and spices as they can totally transform the taste of your meals. Be aware to check the container labels for any sweeteners or MSG that has been added, though.

Black and white pepper

Sea salt

Chili powder

Cayenne pepper

Curry powder

Cumin

Oregano

Rosemary

Thyme

Nutmeg

Cloves

Ginger

Nuts & Seeds

Although these are on your shopping list, you must be aware that they contain Omega 6 fatty acids - so they should be used in moderation as they are easy to overeat and add too much to your carbohydrate intake.

Seeds (sesame, sunflower, and pumpkin)

Nuts (walnuts, pecans, hazelnuts, almonds)

Peanuts are classed as a legume so should be avoided.

Vegetables

With vegetables, it is best to try to stick to green leafy veggies and avoid any root vegetables.

Seaweeds (any type of sea vegetables are suitable)

Peppers

Broccoli

Cucumber

Cabbage

Lettuce

Watercress

Spinach

Shallots

Zucchini

Kimchi

Sauerkraut

Meats

Try to buy cuts of meat that have been grass-fed, or organic to avoid any pesticides or antibiotics that may have been used. All meats are good to eat, but as they are high in protein, so they must be limited so as not to hamper the ketosis process, which is aimed for here.

Pork

Beef

Lamb

Mutton

Goat

Wild Game

Venison

Bacon, hams and sausages (carb count for any of these should be less than 1 gram per serving)

Another category in the meats section is *organ meats,* although not popular with a lot of people, they are one of the most nutritious foods available. The following organs can be eaten from almost any animal, including:

Heart

Liver

Kidney

Tongue

Tripe

Seafood & Shellfish

Any fish or seafood is suitable if it has not been cultivated, as manmade feeds will have been used. These can be in any form either fresh or frozen. Although shellfish is normally a little on the expensive side, the nutrition you gain from it can be worth the little extra cost.

Bass

Cod

Haddock

Halibut

Herring

Mackerel

Tuna

Tilapia

Cod

Trout

Salmon

Shrimp

Scallops

Prawns

Lobster

Clams

Mussels

Oysters

Caviar

Poultry

With poultry or any other fowl, these can be safe to eat in whole or in part. With these, the best option is to find ones that are organically raised, where possible.

Chicken

Turkey

Duck

Dairy Products

Eggs

Greek yoghurt (this should be plain and full fat with a carb count less than 7 per individual serving)

Heavy creams

Sour cream

Cream cheese

Soft cheeses

Cheddar

Parmesan

Fruits

As previously mentioned a lot of fruits must be avoided in large quantities although some fruits are great in moderation.

In season berries (raspberry, strawberry, blueberry and Cranberry, which all have a low sugar content).

Avocados (can be used as a snack or made into guacamole for dipping)

Olives

Lemon

Lime

Legumes

Most legumes must be avoided although in small quantities peas and green beans are fine.

Fats & Oils

The Keto diet is high fat and low carbs, so fats and oils play a major part as they make up the major part of the body's calorie intake. All you must be aware of is the fats you are taking are considered healthy fats, for this plan. Include these:

Olive oils

Avocado oils

Coconut oils

Palm shortening

Duck fat

Sesame oils

Cocoa butter

Butter (if you can tolerate dairy products)

Drinks

As with most drinks, it is better to check the ingredients for any hidden sugars they may contain.

Coconut milk

Almond milk

Tea (both normal and herbal)

Coffee

Sparkling mineral water

Club soda

Water (rain or filtered is always best)

Chapter 5: Yummy Breakfast Recipes

Even though you have decided to take the path to a healthier lifestyle, there is no need to sacrifice what a lot of people regard as the most important meal of the day. I have compiled a list of recipes from simple favorites, to some more heart-warming and exclusive dishes, if you decide you want a special treat.

Mixed Veggie Hash 1 Serving

Prep time: 10 minutes

Overall time: 20-25 minutes

Ingredients

Broccoli	100 grams
Cauliflower	100 grams
Bacon	60 grams
Onion	1 small
Garlic	1 clove
Chives	1 tbsp
Sea Salt	¼ tsp
Avocado	½ medium

Directions:

1. Peel and finely chop your onion and garlic and chives.

2. Slice bacon into small cubes or strips.

3. Put your coconut oil in your pan.

4. Sweat your onion and garlic over medium heat and add your bacon, cook until a light brown color is achieved.

5. Cut your broccoli and cauliflower into medium pieces.

6. Add these to your pan along with the salt and cook for another 10 – 15 minutes or until your vegetables start to become tender.

7. Once plated, top with your sliced avocado and chopped chives, or alternatively, you can substitute the avocado for a fried egg.

Waffles Keto Makes 10

Prep 10 minutes

Overall time   30 – 40 minutes

Ingredients

Eggs	10 separated
Coconut Flour	8 tbsp
Sweetener	3 – 5 tbsp (use your sweetener of choice)
Baking Powder	2 tsp

Vanilla	3 – 4 tsp
Full-Fat Milk	6 tbsp
Butter	250 g (melted)
Fresh Berries	100 grams
Cream	for drizzling

Instructions

Get two separate bowls:

Bowl 1

Whisk the egg whites until firm and peaks form.

Bowl 2

1. Mix egg yolks, coconut flour, baking powder and your sweetener.

2. Slowly add your melted butter and mix to a smooth consistency.

3. Add vanilla and the milk and mix well.

4. Gently fold in the beaten egg whites into yolk mixture keeping as much air in as possible.

5. Fill waffle maker with enough mixture to make your waffle and cook until golden.

6. Serve with a few berries and cream.

Breakfast Omelet with Avocado 4 Servings

Prep time 10 minutes

Overall time 15 minutes

Ingredients

Eggs	4 free range or organic
Cheese	2 oz
Mixed Herbs	1 tsp (use any mixed herbs to your desired taste)
Oil	(MCT oil or coconut oil can be used)
Sea Salt	½ tsp
Avocado	1 medium fruit

Instructions

1. In a large bowl, whisk the eggs with the oil, mixed herbs, and salt until mixture becomes foamy.

2. Peel and slice avocado into medium slices.

3. In a skillet melt the butter on medium-high flame and then cook avocado until golden on both sides then remove and set aside.

4. In your skillet, pour the egg mixture, slice your cheese into thin slices and place it over the egg mixture.

5. Cover the pan and cook until the bottom of the frittata is golden brown.

6. Carefully turn the frittata and cook for another 2 minutes (you may need a plate to help turn the frittata).

Serve the frittata topped with the fried avocado.

Keto Fried Breakfast Serves 2

Prep time 5 minutes

Overall time 15 minutes

Ingredients

Bacon	4 pieces uncured
Avocado	1 large fruit
Eggs	4 medium free range or organic
Sea Salt	¼ tsp
Oil	Coconut oil for cooking

Instructions

1. Heat oil in skillet over medium heat.

2. Place bacon and avocado and cook for 3 minutes or until golden, turn and cook for another few minutes until golden.

3. Remove avocado and bacon and then crack eggs into your pan.

4. Cook eggs to your liking.

5. Remove eggs and serve with bacon and avocado.

Cinnamon Pancake Donuts Makes 20 - 22

Prep time 10 minutes

Overall time 30 minutes

Ingredients

Eggs	3 large
Almond Flour	4 tbsp
Coconut Flour	1 tbsp
Cinnamon	¼ tsp
Baking Powder	1 tsp
Vanilla Extract	1 tsp

Cream Cheese	3 oz
Sweetener	4 tbsp (sweetener of choice)
Coconut oil	for cooking

Instructions

1. Place all ingredients in a bowl and mix with an immersion blender for about 1 minute.

2. Heat donut maker and brush with coconut oil.

3. Fill each well to ¾ full.

4. Cook for 3 minutes on one side then turn and cook for another 2 minutes.

5. Remove from donut maker and repeat until mixture is finished. Serve warm.

BLT Keto Serves 2

Prep time 10 minutes

Overall time 20 minutes

Ingredients

Low Carb Bread	4 pieces
Homemade Mayo	3-4 tbsp
Bacon	6 pieces

Lettuce Leaves	2 large leaves
Tomato	1 large thinly sliced
Basil	1 tbsp fresh

Instructions

1. Fry bacon until golden brown on both sides or more if you like it crispy.

2. Place bread in pan and fry until warm and slightly browned.

3. Remove bread and spread homemade mayo on both top and bottom slice.

4. Layer bacon, lettuce and tomato in layers between two slices of low carb bread.

Eat while still warm and enjoy.

Easy Microwave Muffins Serves 2

Prep time 5 minutes

Overall time 15 minutes

Ingredients

Egg	1 large
Heavy Cream	1 dash
Sweetener	1-2 tsp (sweetener of your choice)

Salt	¼ tsp
Vanilla	1 tsp
Cinnamon	¼ tsp
Flax meal	4 tbsp

Instructions

Mix ingredients in a microwave safe bowl then place into microwave and cook for 1 to 1 1/2 minutes.

If it appears dry - add a small piece of butter on top of the warm muffin and let it soak in.

For alternative flavors, you can add either 1 tbsp of unsweetened cocoa powder or add a few berries of your choice.

Simple Fresh Fruit with Cream Serves 2

A very simple breakfast and very refreshing, choose 1 of the following and drizzle with heavy cream or whipped cream.

Fresh Strawberries	½ cup
Fresh Raspberries	½ cup
Apricot	1 medium
Avocado	½ medium

Peach	1 small or ½ medium

Choco Overnight Pudding Serves 2

Prep time   15 minutes

Ingredients

Almond Milk	240 ml
Chia Seeds	20 grams
Cocoa Powder	12 grams unsweetened
Maple syrup	25 ml
Cinnamon	¼ tsp
Sea Salt	1/8 tsp

Instructions

1. Add all ingredients into a bowl and whisk until a smooth consistency.

2. Check for sweetness and add maple syrup to desired taste.

3. Cover and place in fridge overnight.

Serve chilled and for more flavor, you can add a small number of berries, granola or a nice dollop of whipped cream.

Keto Porridge Serves 4

Prep time 5 minutes

Overall time 10 minutes

Ingredients

Almond flour	12 tbsp
Golden Flax	4 tbsp
Salt	½ tsp
Eggs	4 medium or 3 large
Butter	8 tsp
Sweetener	3-4 tbsp or to taste
Heavy Cream	4 tbsp (coconut milk can also be used)

Instructions

1. Measure ingredients into a small pan and heat on medium.

2. Once mixture starts to simmer, reduce heat and whisk until it thickens.

3. Remove from heat, add beaten eggs a little at a time while whisking. Return to heat until mixture thickens. Once thickened remove from heat and whisk for another 30 – 40 seconds.

4. Add the cream, sweetener and butter and whisk until combined.

5. Add some fresh berries for an added delight.

Chapter 6: Awesome Salads

Salads are one of those meals that everyone loves, they are fresh and tasty and most of all, one of the very easiest and quickest meals to make. While on the Keto diet, there is no reason for you to have any sacrifices in any salad.

Tuna Salad Serves 2

Prep time 15 minutes

Overall time 20 minutes

Ingredients

Tuna	1 can (make sure it is in brine or vegetable oil)
Bacon	2 slice
Onion	1 tbsp chopped
Sour Cream	1 tbsp
Mustard	2 tsp (any you like but Dijon gives best taste)
Dill	¼ tsp
Eggs	2 medium boiled and chopped
Mayo	1 tbsp homemade

Instructions

1. Fry bacon for 3 minutes on either side or until your liking.

2. Drain tuna and place in small bowls, then add chopped egg and chopped onion.

3. Add remaining ingredients and mix well.

4. Top with crumbled bacon and serve.

Thai Chicken Serves 2

Prep time 15 minutes

Overall Time 20 minutes

Ingredients

Chicken Breast	2 boneless and skinless
Garlic	2 cloves crushed
Lime Juice	3 tbsp
Sea Salt	¼ tsp
Pepper	1/8 tsp
Spring Onion	1 small bunch
Red Bell Pepper	1 thinly sliced
Zucchini	either yellow or green and julienned

Red Curry Paste	1 ½ tsp
Rice Noodles	enough for 2 servings

Salad Dressing

Olive Oil	2 tbsp
Lime juice	2 tbsp
Cilantro	1 tbsp finely chopped
Garlic	2 cloves crushed
Coconut Palm Sugar	2 tsp
Fish Sauce	1 tbsp

Instructions

1. Slice chicken breasts into even pieces.

2. Combine garlic, lime juice, salt and pepper.

3. Coat chicken pieces in the garlic and lime juice marinade, cover and place in the fridge for between 30 minutes to 1 hour.

4. Remove chicken from fridge and grill on high for 5 – 6 minutes on either side or until chicken is cooked all the way through.

5. Cook rice noodles as per packet instructions.

6. As your chicken is cooking add the olive oil, lime juice, cilantro, garlic, sugar and fish sauce to a small bowl. Mix well until it is all combined.

7. Once chicken is cooked, remove from the pan and slice into even bite sized pieces

To serve, place noodles into a bowl and cover with chicken pieces, sprinkle the peppers, zucchini and spring onions over your chicken and then drizzle some of the dressing over the top.

Crunchy Veggie Salad 1-2 Servings

Prep time 10 minutes

Ingredients

Cucumber	½ medium size
Zucchini	½ medium size
Cherry Tomato	10 halved
Spring Onion	2 sliced
Bell Pepper	½ large pepper diced
Radish	4 diced
Lettuce	any medium sized and any type you prefer
Eggs	2 hard boiled

Salt & Pepper	to taste
Basil	1 tsp dry or fresh
Lettuce	½ medium
Watercress	½ bunch

Salad Dressing

Any homemade dressing depending on taste.

Instructions

1. Chop all your veggies and add these to a large bowl and then cover with your favorite dressing and the basil.

2. Mix well to coat everything.

3. Lay washed lettuce and watercress on your plates and then cover with your veggie mixture.

4. Quarter your boiled eggs and arrange on your plates then season with salt and pepper.

Italian Chicken Salad Serves 4

Prep time 20 minutes

Overall time 30 minutes

Ingredients

Chicken Breast	750 grams skinned and boneless
Bell Peppers	2 grilled or roasted
Arugula	3 oz
Celery	½ cup chopped
Basil	¼ cup chopped
Onions	1/3 cup chopped
Avocado Oil	¼ cup
White wine vinegar	¼ cup
Mustard	1 tbsp any type preferred.

Instructions

1. Boil chicken breast for about 20 minutes then remove from heat to cool. Once cooled chop into small even slices.

2. On griddle pan, cook bell peppers until nicely charred and once cooled remove the skins and seeds.

3. Chop the veggies celery, onions, basil and the skinless bell peppers.

4. Mix chicken into veggie mixture.

5. Lay arugula onto plates and divide the chicken veggie mix between them.

Spinach with Bacon Salad Serves 2

Baby Spinach Leaves	3 cups
Rocket	1 ½ cups
Red Onion	1 medium sliced
Blue Cheese	4 – 6 tablespoons
Bacon	2 pieces cooked crispy
Salad Dressing	2 spoons of homemade

Instructions

1. Divide washed spinach & rocket leaves between plates.

2. Lay sliced onion over the top.

3. Sprinkle over the crispy bacon bits and the blue cheese.

Avocado Salad Serves 2

Prep time 15 minutes

Overall time 25minutes

Ingredients

Bacon	4 slices chopped
Avocados	2 peeled, pitted & cubed
Green onions	3 finely chopped
Sour Cream	½ cup
Lemon Juice	1 tbsp
Sea Salt	to taste
Lettuce	1 medium
Watercress	½ bunch

Instructions

1. Cook chopped bacon in skillet until crisp.

2. In a large bowl gently add the avocados, bacon bits, onions, sour cream, lemon juice and salt.

3. Arrange salad leaves on plates and spoon the avocado mixture on top.

Asparagus Salad Serves 4

Prep time 10 minutes

Overall time 30 minutes

Ingredients

Asparagus	500 grams
Shrimp	250 grams
Olive oil	¼ cup
Garlic	2 cloves
Lemon Juice	1 tbsp
Parsley	2 tbsp minced fresh
Salt & Pepper	to taste

Instructions

1. Bring medium pot of water to boil and salt it well, add asparagus and boil for 3 minutes. Remove and allow to cool.

2. Add shrimp to the boiling water and cook for 2-3 minutes, if pre-cooked remove after 30 seconds.

3. Slice asparagus diagonally into thin strips and place in bowl with the shrimp.

4. Add the remaining ingredients and toss to combine, add salt and pepper to taste.

Broccoli Salad Serves 2

Prep time 15 minutes

Overall time 30 minutes

Ingredients

Bacon	4 slices
Broccoli	1 head chopped
Cheddar Cheese	1 cup grated
Red onion	1/2 large
Red wine vinegar	1/8 cup
Sweetener	1 tbsp
Black Pepper	1/2 teaspoon ground
Salt	½ tsp
Mayonnaise	½ cup homemade (Greek yoghurt can be substituted)
Lemon Juice	1 tsp

Instructions

1. Place bacon in skillet and cook until golden brown on both sides, let cool and then crumble.

2. In a bowl combine the broccoli, cheese, onion and bacon bits.

3. In a small bowl mix the red wine vinegar, sweetener, salt, pepper, lemon juice and homemade mayo. Mix well and then combine with the broccoli cheese mixture.

4. Cover and place in refrigerator until ready to serve.

Chapter 7: Beautiful Main Meals

This is what we all look forward to, getting home and putting our feet up and having a nice hearty meal after a long day. These recipes I have compiled should satisfy most taste buds. They range from my own favorites too other yummy 'must try's.'

Chicken Tikka Masala Serves 2

Ingredients

Chicken Breast	2 medium
Onion Powder	1 tsp
Garlic	2 cloves minced
Ginger	1 inch grated or finely chopped
Garam Masala	3 tsp
Tomato Paste	2 tbsp (unsweetened)
Paprika	1 tsp
Sea Salt	2 tsp
Diced Tomatoes	1 10 oz. can (unsweetened)
Fresh Cilantro	chopped for topping
Coconut Milk	3/4 cup
Heavy Cream	3/4 cup

Olive Oil	2 tbsp
Guar Gum	1 tsp

Instructions

1. Cut chicken breast into bite size pieces and add to slow cooker.

2. Add all the dry spices and the grated ginger and mix into chicken pieces.

3. Add tomato paste and canned tomatoes.

4. Add half of the coconut milk and stir well to combine all and then cook on low for approx. 6 hours.

5. Once cooked add the guar gum, cream and the remaining coconut milk.

Serve warm with your vegetables of choice.

Nutted Fish Serves 2

Prep Time 15 minutes

Overall time 30 minutes

Ingredients

Fish Fillets of Choice	2 x 3 oz fillets
Olive Oil	1 tbsp

Salt & Pepper	to taste
Dill	½ tsp
Maple Syrup	2 tbsp unsweetened
Walnuts	½ cup crushed
Mustard	½ tbsp Dijon or other preferred

Instructions

1. Heat oven to 350 degrees F.

2. Add mustard, walnuts, spices and maple syrup to your food processor and blend until you have a smooth consistency.

3. Heat skillet until hot, add your fish fillets skin side down, let it sear for about 3 minutes.

4. While searing, cover the top of the fillet with your spice mixture.

5. Once seared transfer to the oven and bake for 8 minutes.

King Chicken Serves 2

Chicken Thighs	2 x medium with bone and skin on
Salt & pepper	to taste
Almonds	¼ cup (other nuts can be used, avoid peanuts)
Green Pepper	½ medium
Spring Onions	½ bunch
Birds Eye Chili	2 de-seeded

Sauce Mix

Soy Sauce	1 tbsp
Sweetener	to taste
Maple extract	½ tsp
Sesame Oil	2 tsp
Ketchup	1 tbsp reduced sugar
Chili Garlic Paste	2 tbsp
Rice Wine Vinegar	2 tsp

Instructions

1. Cut chicken into bite sized pieces then season with salt and pepper and the ginger.

2. Heat skillet over medium high heat, once hot add chicken and cook for about 10 minutes until browned.

3. Chop veggies and place in a bowl.

4. Prepare the sauce and put aside.

5. Once chicken is cooked, add veggies and nuts then cook for a further 3 minutes.

6. Add sauce to the pan and let it reduce slightly until slightly sticky. Serve hot.

Chicken Nuggets Serves 2

Preparation Time 15 minutes

Overall Time 30 minutes

Ingredients

Chicken	12 oz chicken thigh
Egg	1 medium
Pork Rinds	1 oz

Almond Meal	1/8 cup
Flaxseed Meal	1/8 cup
Lime Zest	½ of 1 lime
Sea Salt	1/8 tsp
Cheese Powder	1 tsp
Cloves	1 pinch
Pepper	1/8 tsp
Chili Powder	1/8 tsp
Paprika	1/8 tsp
Onion Powder	1/8 tsp
Garlic Powder	1/8 tsp
Cayenne Pepper	1/8 tsp

Dipping Sauce

Mayonnaise	½ Cup Homemade
Avocado	½ Medium
Chili Flakes	½ tsp
Lime Juice	1 tbsp
Garlic Powder	¼ tsp

Cumin   1/8 tsp

Instructions

1. Heat Oven to 400 degrees F. Dry chicken thigh and cut into bite size pieces.

2. Add to food processor the spices, lime zest, pork rinds almond meal and flax meal. Pulse until the mixture looks like fine bread crumbs.

3. Pour these into another bowl and then crack 1 egg into another bowl and whisk until the yolk and white is combined. You may have to add a few drops of water to help this happen.

4. Dredge your chicken pieces through the egg mixture and then roll in the spice mix, once coated place onto a foil lined cookie sheet that has been lightly oiled.

5. Bake until nuggets are golden brown on top and the meat is cooked all the way through.

6. While nuggets are cooling, combine ingredients for the sauce and mix well.

Ginger Pork Serves 4 - 6

Preparation Time 15

Overall Time 30

Ingredients

Pork leg	700 grams of boneless shoulder or
Ginger	2 ½ inch peeled and sliced
Chilies	2-3 finger length deseeded
Shallots	3
Coconut Oil	2 tbsp
Kaffir Lime Leaves	5
Turmeric	2 (optional)
Lemongrass inner and slice	3 stalks, use bottom third only bruise
Sea Salt	½ tsp

Instructions

1. Cut pork into bite sized chunks.

2. In food processor add ginger, chilies and shallots with a little water, pulse until a paste forms.

3. Heat oil in skillet over medium heat and stir fry the ground paste mixture until fragrant 3 – 5 minutes.

4. Add pork and remaining ingredients and stir fry for about 2 minutes then reduce heat to low setting, cover pan and simmer until tender about 5 minutes. Add warm water if the gravy starts to dry.

Special Fried Chicken Serves 4 - 6

Preparation Time 40 minutes

Overall time 60 minutes

Ingredients

Coconut Oil	for frying
Salam Leaves	2
Chicken	1 whole chicken about 1kg in weight
Coconut milk	2 cups
Limes	2 cut into wedges for serving
Sambal Trasi	
Spice Paste	
Coriander seeds	1 tbsp or 2 tsp ground coriander
Galangal (Ginger)	½ inch peeled and sliced

Turmeric Powder	¾ tsp
Ginger	2cm peeled and sliced
Shallots	4-5 peeled
Garlic	3 cloves peeled
Brown Sugar	1 tbsp
Sea Salt	¼ teaspoon

Instructions

1. Add spice paste ingredients to food processor with a little oil and pulse until a smooth paste forms.

2. Heat a skillet over medium heat and add 2 tbsp oil when hot then stir fry the spice paste until fragrant, 3 – 5 minutes Add chicken and stir fry to coat all the pieces with the sauce.

3. Add coconut milk and bring to the boil then reduce heat and simmer uncovered until the sauce has nearly dried and the chicken is almost cooked, for about 20 minutes.

4. Just before serving, heat oil in pan until very hot and then deep fry your chicken pieces until crisp and brown about 3 minutes.

Spinach Soup Serves 2

Preparation time 10 minutes

Overall time 30 minutes

Ingredients

Fresh Spinach	5 oz trimmed
Chicken Broth	2 cups
Onion	1/2 medium chopped
Garlic	4 cloves minced
Salt	1/4 tsp
Butter	1/4 cup
Soy Flour	1/8 cup
Heavy Cream	1/3 cup
Water	1/8 cup
Pepper	1/4 tsp
Nutmeg	1 pinch

Instructions

1. Add the spinach, broth and carrots and bring to a boil, reduce the heat and simmer for 5 minutes stirring occasionally.

2. Remove from heat and allow to cool until warm.

3. In a skillet on medium high melt butter, sauté the onion and garlic until soft about 7 minutes, add soy flour and cook over low heat for 3 - 5 minutes. Add spinach mix.

4. Once cooked add small batches to blender and pulse until finely chopped. return to a large pan, add cream, water nutmeg and pepper and re-heat but do not boil.

Turkey Broccoli Casserole Serves 4

Prep time 20 minutes

Overall time 40 minutes

Broccoli	1 x 5 oz pack frozen
Turkey Breast	1 cup cooked and diced
Mushroom Soup	1/2 10 oz can cream of mushroom
Heavy Cream	1/4 cup
Cheddar Cheese	1/4 cup grated

Instructions

1. Preheat oven to 375 degrees F.

2. Cook broccoli according to package details and then layer in a 12 x 8-inch baking dish.

3. Layer the cooked diced turkey breast over the top.

4. Add the cream to the soup and mix until well combined.

5. Pour the soup mix over the turkey and cover with the grated cheese.

6. Bake for 30 minutes and let cool for 5 minutes before serving.

Chicken Sour Bake Serves 4

Ingredients

Chicken Breast	1kg
Oat Flour	½ cup
Sea Salt	1 tsp
Pepper	¼ tsp
Coconut Oil	¼ cup
Heavy Cream	½ cup
Sour Cream	1 cup
Dried Onion Soup Mix	3tbsp

Instructions

1. Slice chicken breasts into thick strips.

2. Mix salt and pepper into flour.

3. Cover chicken strips with flour mixture.

4. Heat oil in skillet over medium heat, add chicken and brown on all sides.

Mix flour, salt and pepper. Dredge chicken through flour mixture.

5. Place cooked chicken strips into 13 x 9-inch pan.

6. Combine heavy cream, sour cream and dried onion soup mix into a small pan, cook until hot but not boiling.

7. Pour mixture over chicken cover and bake at 350 degrees F for 1 hour or until tender.

Chapter 8: Tempting Snacks & Desserts

I know you are thinking, I am going to miss out on a lot of enjoyable foods and I will get hungry between meals. That can be the case - but in this chapter I hope to give you some snacks that can stave off hunger between meals, and a few desserts that will complete your evening meal and make you feel totally satisfied.

Coated Goat Cheese makes 6 - 8

Ingredients

Goat Cheese	1 x 4 oz packaged sundried tomato goat cheese
Pistachios	½ cup shelled and chopped or crushed
Salt	to taste

Instructions

1. Cut cheese into equal sizes and form into balls.

2. Crush or finely chop your nuts and add salt to taste.

3. Roll balls of goat cheese into nut mixture to coat.

Peanut Butter Snacks Makes 12 - 16

Ingredients

Butter	2 stick unsalted
Unsweetened Chocolate	2 oz
Sweetener	2/3 cup sweetener of choice
Heavy Cream	4 tbsp
Walnuts	¼ cup chopped (optional)
Peanut butter	8 tbsp

Instructions

1. Place chocolate and butter in a double boiler, heat until both have fully combined.

2. Add powdered sweetener and mix until fully melted.

3. Once melted, add cream and peanut butter and stir until combined, taste and adjust if needed.

4. Line muffin tins with liners and sprinkle a few nuts in the bottom and divide the peanut butter mixture between the cups.

5. Place in freezer until firm. Note store in freezer as they melt quickly.

Bacon Cheese Rolls Makes 10

Preparation time 15 minutes

Ingredients

Mozzarella Cheese	4 oz
Almond Flour	2 tbsp
Butter	2 tbsp melted
Flaxseed Powder	1 ½ tbsp.
Egg	1 medium
Sea Salt	1/8 tsp
Ground Black pepper	1/8 tsp
Garlic Powder	1/8 tsp
Onion Powder	1/8 tsp
Bacon	5 slices
Coconut Oil	for frying

Instructions

1. Grate mozzarella and add half (2 oz) to a medium microwave bowl, melt until soft and stringy.

2. Melt butter and add to cheese.

3. Add egg to mixture and mix well.

4. Add almond flour and flaxseed powder and the remainder of the spices.

5. After mixing, turn out onto surface and form a large rectangle and spread remainder of cheese over half of rectangle.

6. Pinch all the edges so there are no open spots.

7. Using a sharp knife cut into squares.

8. Cut bacon in halves and put one of the squares at one end.

9. Roll bacon around mixture until the end can overlap.

10. Use toothpick to stabilize it.

11. Heat oil in pan to 350f and fry the cubes until golden on all sides.

Eggs with Avocado Makes 4

Preparation Time 5 minutes

Overall 20 minutes

Ingredients

Eggs   2 boiled eggs organic or free range

Avocado	½ pitted and peeled
Goat Cheese	1 tsp
Lime Juice	½ lime
Olive Oil	1 tsp chili infused preferable
Sea Salt	1 pinch
Chili chopped finely	½ small if not using chili infused oil,

Instructions

1. Peel boiled eggs and cut in half.

2. Remove yolks and place in bowl, mix with olive oil, goats cheese and lime juice until a smooth texture is obtained.

3. Peel and remove seed from avocado, mix half of the avocado into the egg yolk mix.

4. Spoon avocado egg mix back into the egg whites carefully.

Keto Brownies Makes 1

Almond Butter	1 tbsp
Egg White	1 large egg, fully beaten
Cocoa Powder	1 tsp
Vanilla	1/8 tsp

Liquid Sweetener	3 drops
Baking Soda	1 small pinch, omit for a denser brownie
Salt	1 pinch

Instructions

1. Beat egg whites until foamy.

2. Add all ingredients to a mug and mix together with a fork.

3. Microwave for 40 seconds (trial and error depending on microwave).

For a gooey Brownie cook for 30 seconds.

These can be topped with anything you like to give you an extra smile.

Nut Coated Goat Cheese makes 6 - 8

Ingredients

Goat Cheese	1 x 4oz packaged goat cheese
Pistachios crushed	½ cup shelled and chopped or
Salt	to taste

Instructions

1. Cut cheese into equal sizes and form into balls.

2. Crush or finely chop your nuts and add salt to taste.

3. roll balls of goat cheese into nut mixture to coat.

Lemon Lime Logs Makes 10

Preparation Time 15 minutes

Overall Time 30 minutes

Ingredients

Sweetener	2-4 tbsp sweetener of choice
Vanilla Extract	1 tsp
Eggs	4 large
Yoghurt unsweetened	¼ cup Greek yoghurt or natural
Almond Flour	½ cup
Coconut Flour	½ cup
Lemon Juice	1 1/2 tbsp
Lemon Zest	1 tbsp
Lime Juice	1 ½ tbsp
Lime Zest	1 tbsp

Salt	1 pinch
Butter	1 stick at room temperature

Lemon Topping

Sweetener	4 tbsp
Lemon Juice	1 ½ tbsp
Lime Juice	1 ½ tbsp

Instructions

1. Heat Oven to 350 degrees F.

2. Mix the coconut flour and almond flour.

3. Mix the sweetener with the softened butter and add the eggs one by one, mix until you have a consistent mix.

4. Slowly add the flour a little at a time until it is fully incorporated.

5. Add the lemon and lime juice and then the yoghurt, finally add the lemon & lime zest and mix until everything is combined.

6. Line and grease a baking tray, pour mixture in and level with a spatula.

7. Cook for 15-20 minutes or until a toothpick comes out clean in the center.

8. While cooking, mix the lemon and lime juice with the powdered sweetener.

9. When removed from oven allow to cool and pour the topping and then cut into logs/bars.

Easy Nut Fudge Serves 4

Preparation time 10 minutes

Overall time 20 minutes

Ingredients

Unsweetened coco powder	¼ cup
Peanut butter	1 cup unsweetened
Coconut Oil	1 cup
Almond milk	plain or vanilla flavor
Salt	1 pinch
Sweetener	to taste

Instructions

1. Mix coconut oil and peanut butter together over low heat.

2. In a blender add this to your other ingredients.

3. Blend until fully combined.

4. Line & grease a loaf pan.

5. Pour mixture into loaf pan and level with a spatula.

6. Place in refrigerator, approx. 2 hours to set.

7. Cut into bite size pieces and return to refrigerator for storing.

Strawberry Cream Popsicles

Strawberry Layer

Strawberries	2 cups
Lemon Juice	2 tbsp
Sweetener	to taste

Cream Layer

Coconut Milk	13.5 oz
Vanilla Extract	½ tsp
Sweetener	to taste

Instructions

1. Blend strawberries, lemon juice and sweetener until a mushy consistency.

2. Mix coconut milk, sweetener and vanilla extract in another bowl.

3. Partially fill popsicle mold 1/3 full.

4. Add coconut milk on top of strawberry mixture until 2/3 from the top.

5. Spoon more strawberry mixture and top the mold with more coconut milk mixture if needed.

6. Place in freezer overnight or for at least 6 hours.

Mixed Berry Surprise Makes 12

Raspberries	150 grams fresh or frozen
Strawberries	150 grams fresh or frozen
Vanilla	1 tsp
Heavy Cream	200 grams (to be whipped)
Gelatine	24 grams
Sweetener	12 grams
Greek Yoghurt	750 grams of full fat

Topping

Strawberries	1 tbsp
Raspberries	1 tbsp
Sweetener	2 tbsp
Cream Cheese	125 grams (can also use mascarpone cheese if available)

Instructions

Line a spring form pan with parchment paper, both on the bottom and around the inside.

1. Mix sweetener and yoghurt in a bowl.

2. Dissolve gelatin in ¼ cup of hot water & add 6 tablespoons of yoghurt mixture, mix well until sweetener is dissolved.

3. Pour gelatin mix into bowl with the remaining yoghurt.

4. Whip cream and carefully fold into the yoghurt gelatin mix.

5. Remove 1 tbsp of strawberries and raspberries.

6. Fold remaining berries into yoghurt mixture.

Coco-Bounty Bars Makes 10

Ingredients

Shredded Coconut	2 cup unsweetened
Sweetener	4 teaspoons or adjust for taste
Cocoa Powder	4 tbsp Unsweetened
Vanilla Extract	2 tsp
Coconut Oil	8 tbsp
Coconut Cream	2/3 cup

Instructions

1. In a large bowl mix coconut cream with half of the vanilla extract and the shredded coconut, check for sweetness and add sweetener as desired.

2. Place coconut mixture on a small lined baking tray and shape it into a rectangular shape roughly 6 inch by 4 inch and about 1 inch thick.

3. Place in freezer until solid, 2-3 hours' minimum, remove and cut into 10 bars.

Chocolate Coating

4. In a small saucepan mix coconut oil, add cocoa powder and the left over sweetener and vanilla. Heat on low for about 2 minutes stirring occasionally.

5. Remove from heat and let cool to room temperature.

6. Dip each frozen bar in chocolate mix covering all sides, once covered return bars to baking tray.

7. Once all are coated return to refrigerator.

Best stored in refrigerator, coating will easily melt if it is left in room temperature.

Conclusion

While every attempt has been made to include as much information as possible in this book regarding the Keto diet, the individual is always encouraged to seek added information; medical advice if required. As with most diets the main questions are, "will it do me good," or "will it be bad?" And, is it another diet that is just following a trend and trying to be hip?

The idea behind the Keto diet was conceived in the early 1920's and its main aim was to help epilepsy sufferers, which in itself it cannot be a bad thing. Constant results keep showing how you can benefit from following the Keto Diet for weight loss and general health.

Throughout the book, you will notice the majority of the content is focused on the recipes, where there is a variation of real meals, with easy ingredients to find. There may be one or two abstract ingredients - but there is a good possibility these can be substituted from something that is in your local supermarket, or area. Thank you so much for reading this book, I sincerely hope it gives you every success in the future with your weight loss or health based program. Please remember to NEVER use the Keto diet on children, because they are still growing, and should have a balanced diet that is low in sugar, with lots of veggies, fruit and proteins (found in meats and fish). Thank you.

www.ingramcontent.com/pod-product-compliance
Lightning Source LLC
Chambersburg PA
CBHW021440170526
45164CB00001B/322